The Malaise of the Malayalees

Dr. John Mathew

(Sunny Ezhumattoor)

Published By
Thekkel Publications a
Division of Narrow Path Ministries
Web address: www.Thekkel.com
www.NarrowPathMinitries.net

ISBN: 9798390861196

Table of Contents

Introduction

"Our Father who is in heaven,
Hallowed be Thy name.
Your kingdom come,
Thy will be done,
On earth as it is in heaven.
Give us this day our daily bread.
And forgive us our debts, as we also have forgiven our
debtors.
And lead us not to temptation but deliver us from evil."
Matthew 6:9-13 (NASB)

In the Lord's model prayer quoted above, Jesus is teaching His disciples and subsequently all His followers down through the centuries, to have an eager anticipation and longing for God's kingdom to be established on the earth. He teaches us to pray, "Thy kingdom come." This new kingdom is our most pressing need ever since the original perfect kingdom was lost when sin entered the Garden. The great English Poet John Milton, in his epic poem 'Paradise Lost', describes his dilemma over the loss of the perfect Paradise. He writes.

Of Man's First Disobedience, and the Fruit
Of that Forbidden Tree, whose mortal taste
Brought Death into the World, and all our woe,
With loss of Eden, till one greater Man
Restore us and regain the blissful Seat.
[Paradise Lost 1:1]

John Milton was driven by the ideals of the Puritanical teachings and had anchored his faith in the

Lord Jesus Christ for restoring the perfect order that was lost at the beginning of human race. Although became blind in his later years, Milton envisioned a 'perfect Paradise' when the chaos of this universe will disappear, and thereby a new dawn will bless the ones who wait for that 'kingdom to come.' As we move through the centuries and supposedly improving the standards of humanity with technological advancements and other sociological innovations, yet we sadly observe that the humanity is still controlled by fallen humans and will invariably go from bad to worse. This book that you are about to read will remain as a testament to this eternal truth.

The author of this book, "The Malaise of the Malayalees," Dr. Sunny Ezhumattoor," is well known as a writer of Christian and secular books for the past several decades in the North America and parts of India as well as other places. He had displayed a keen sense of observation to capture the peculiarities of various cultures and had presented here in this book, an educational tool to many curious minds. The articles contained in this book had the appearance of a 'coat of many colors' which keeps the attention of the readers to be pleasantly engaged and conjoined with the ideas of the author. The general observations citing various peculiarities and unique traits, primarily are of the 'Malayalee' communities, but may not necessarily to be restrictive only among them. These are of universal level especially now as the world is closely connected from continent to continent more than ever. Such behavioral intricacies are greatly affecting the public's life and thus creating a cesspool of misery to all. They are portrayed in this book very vividly. To understand the nuances of what all are addressed in this book, one must have closer ties with the Kerala or Malayalee culture and practices. The author is immersing us into the history of Kerala to get a fresher look at the impact many of the political leaders of yesteryear had on this tiny state. Their political allegiance and fascination to communism weighed down heavily on ordinary people and drowned their aspirations to become contributors among the local communities. Instead, they found their worth in other parts of India or elsewhere.

Let me go back to the Lord's model prayer from Matthew 6 and John Milton's lines Our only hope of deliverance is solidly resting on this line – 'Thy kingdom come.' We all look forward to reaching the kingdom that the 'One greater Man' who had restored for us and has now occupied that 'blissful Seat.' By faith in Jesus' finished work we reach there, not based on our merit but on His merit of being sinless and a perfect sacrifice for our sins. My prayer is that this book would remain as a constant reminder for all its readers that we live in a fallen world, as the author puts in Chapter 5, and those who have received the light of the gospel to illumine the path for the rest as a beacon of light.

As a friend of Dr. Sunny Ezhumattoor and being at the same home Assembly of Ezhumattoor from our childhood days, I am delighted that he asked me to comment on this book and make some introductory remarks. May God graciously give us eternal wisdom and guidance as we strive each day to be in His service.

Tom Johns,
Dallas, Texas

1

The Malaise of Malayalees

(A Critical Review)

I am going to provide some examples of negative behavioral patterns of most Malayalees based on my sociological observations. In the past in many essays, I have portrayed many positive aspects of Malayalees. This study is like a one side of a coin. Here I portray the dark side. I reluctantly became a unique "social martyr "through this work. Basic human behavior is the same all over the world. However, on economic system like socialism and peculiar cultures, can create strange types of behavior. The Indian population has a general behavior pattern, however, the Malayalees took that peculiar behavior to an extreme level. I hope eventually Malayalees will transform and become more civilized.

Nobody wants to antagonize the readers and then try to appease them. This work may look incoherent because the whole work doesn't speak of a particular subject. You see the discontinuity because this essay unravels the psychological, social, economic, and political behavior of a community. It deals with various and total aspects of Malayalee behavior.

Sthālīpulākanyāya (स्थालीपुलाकन्याय). (Cooking Pot and Boiled Rice)

"The maxim of the cooking-pot and the boiled rice. In a cooking-pot all the grains are equally moistened by the heated water and so, when one knows that one grain is well-cooked, he can draw the same inference as regards to all others. From this fact the maxim is applied to cases where the condition of the whole is inferred from that of a part."

Malayalees can be seen in every nook and corner of the world. They are the most adventurous people under the sun. Syrian Christians in Kerala started the great migration in the early 1950 s. They started to go to Malaysia and Singapore. In the sixties they started to go to Africa as teachers. They also went to the Middle East for jobs. Then Kerala Hindus and Muslims also followed that pattern. There is a joke about the Malayalee. "When Neil Armstrong went to the moon in 1969, he saw a Malayalee Coffee shop there!"

It is prudent to ask why everyone in Kerala wants to leave as soon as they get a chance. Kerala was the only place in the world that elected a communist government in 1957. Even in 2023, the Communists are in power in Kerala. What about other parties? All Kerala parties and politicians are like cobras. The only difference is that Marxists have inflated hoods that hiss and spit. Other parties are like regular cobras without raised hoods. In the states of Tamil Nadu and Kerala many parents name their children Stalin and Lenin. At present the chief Minister of Tamil Nadu is M.K. Stalin

In Kerala there are many Stalin and Lenin among Kerala Brethren. Now no one in the former Soviet Union and China name their children Lenin and Stalin. It seems that Malayalees have a special Socialist DNA. Most Indians hate the White man and America. For further details read my book on "Conspiracy Theories" from Amazon.

In January 2023, a think Tank took a survey among Indians and found most Indians view. Most Indians consider America as a threat after China.

Indians forget that American technology makes their life easy and comfortable. All these technologies are free. Anyone can make a video call free of charge with WhatsApp and any other dozen companies. GPS and all other technologies make their lives better; however, America is their great villain. In my childhood, a person who made an average salary just to survive. After American companies outsourced their manufacturing in India, the Indian worker can live a luxurious life.

The following news report confirms my repeated statements about the hatred and prejudice against America by most Indians.

Indians View U.S as the Biggest Threat after China, Survey Shows

By Eltaf Najafizada

Bloomberg News • January 18, 2023

(Tribune News Service) — Indians view the U.S. as the biggest military threat after China and place a greater blame on NATO and Washington, than on Russian President Vladimir Putin for his war in Ukraine, according to a new survey.

Some 43 percent of the 1,000 respondents perceived China — with whom India has a long-lingering border dispute and has seen tensions flare again since 2020 — as the greatest threat, according to the survey by Morning Consult, a U.S.-based global business intelligence company.

However, 22 percent saw the U.S. as the second-most significant security threat, ahead of India's historic arch-rival Pakistan, the survey showed.

"While the world's two largest democracies would seem to make for natural partners, especially given their mutual mistrust of China, Indians have strategic reasons to be wary of the world's Western superpower," according to Sonnet Frisbie and Scott Moskowitz, who oversaw the survey released on Tuesday.

India has remained neutral on the Russian war in Ukraine despite pressure from its Quad partners — refraining from U.N. censure votes, while urging a diplomatic solution to ease the food and fertilizer crunch triggered by the crisis. It has also continued to snap up cheap Russian oil.

More Indians blame the U.S. and NATO for the war because "Historical ties with Russia formed during the Cold War and India's post-independence period run deeper than India's relatively new relationship with the U.S.," said Shumita Deveshwar, India research senior director at TS Lombard. Russia, as the main supplier of weapons and cheap oil to India is also "embedded in the mindset of the people, and that takes much longer to change."

New Delhi and Moscow have a long-standing relationship that spans such sectors as defense and security. India is the world's largest buyer of Russian weapons, and a surge in oil purchases by Asia's second-biggest importer has helped the Kremlin to maintain exports as it tackles Western sanctions.

©2023 Bloomberg L.P."

Nokku Kooli (demanding money for just looking at the merchandise, without working)

Most Malayalees think that they are born leaders. I have conducted a lot of research on the sociological behavior patterns of many races and tribes in the world. I am providing a few facts about a typical Malayalee. Many in Kerala claim that they are the most intelligent people on earth. Yes, it is true that the literacy rate in Kerala is one of the highest in the world. Once Kerala achieved a 100 percent literacy rate. However, their behavior proves that they are the most educated barbarians in the world. **"True education is the education of the heart."** I can provide many examples to prove my point about the extreme degenerate mind of Malayalees. Even Amazon jungle Tribals have a better conscience than these Marxist leeches.

The above harsh statement is only applicable to people who practice Nokku Kooli

Nokku Kooli (demanding money for just looking at the merchandise, without working)

This is from Wikipedia "Nokku kooli is a euphemism for extortion by organized labor unions in Kerala under which bribes are paid to trade union activists in exchange for allowing unaffiliated workers to unload their own belongings and materials. This happens with the tacit support of political parties including those in government."

The state of Kerala has monopolized a bad spotlight owing to this act of workers involved in demanding daily wages for doing zero work. Primarily, it involves the headload workers. They are employed to load and unload goods from a vehicle, for which they get paid. However, when the process requires heavy machines instead of human labor, it provides the laborer with an opportunity to protest the employers, claiming they were denied a job. In March 2018, after convening a meeting with all trade unions, Kerala Chief Minister Pinarayi Vijayan declared that the state will be free of nokku kooli (gawking charges) from May 1, 2018. In addition, Pinarayi Vijayan also ordered individuals, private companies, and offices to hire their own staff for the head-loading work. He claimed that unions cannot forcibly take up head-loading work unless they have been hired to do it. Here is a comment by a concerned citizen, Shakthi Velu, "This is a stupid thing that happens ONLY in Kerala." The business community suffers a lot because of this. In this competitive world, even with a low cash flow, they must survive in the market. But this group of workers who are into loading and unloading work will demand their money (Nokku Kooli), even though they do not touch the load. The government is a muted spectator. This is the attitude of the workers across Kerala, to get free money from the bleeding businesses. The funny thing is that they cannot even handle such heavy loads. But they say it is their job that has been snatched away by using machinery. Everyone wants free money and pain-free jobs, which is why no company is ready to invest in Kerala. They look at everything from the outside. Hence, sensible Keralites fly off abroad to live a decent life. The same people work like dogs and donkeys in the Gulf countries. There, if they ask for nokku kooli, the Arab employers will pluck their eyes and ask, "Now u see…?". Kerala is a beautiful state and has a lot to offer, but the so-called unions will have to change their ideas to let it prosper. At least, for the sake of the next generation, the political parties must come forward to stop this extortion of money in the name of Unions."

High Self-Evaluation (Narcissism)

Most Malayalees think that they are born leaders. They are born to be for the pulpit. Many have not figured out their talents. For example, many think that they are good singers and try to sing in public, but sometimes the cacophonous sound becomes unbearable for the audience. They push their children on the stage to do the same without assessing their talents. If you ask them to pray, they may pray for ten to fifteen minutes after making a short statement. If the moderator gives 10 minutes to a Malayalee speaker, he usually takes 25 minutes. Most of them are suffering from a constipation of ideas and diarrhea of words. The second generation Keralites have inherited some traits of their parents.

Here is one great example: Attending a Malayalee funeral service can be a curse and an excruciating experience. For a person with diabetes or other illnesses, participation can bring many sufferings, even hospitalization. First, they conduct a service in their home. It may last around two hours. Later the service will move to the Church.

Most services end in severe crises. Although the organizers want to complete the funeral service in three hours, it may last four to five hours. Everyone wants to say something about the deceased. Usually, the moderator begs the speakers to take only two minutes, however, most take five to ten. The only exception, as far as I know, was at my mother's funeral in 2001. I vetoed the service at home, and the church program lasted only two hours and thirty minutes. Dozens of famous preachers came, but my goal was for the glory of Jesús, and not to satisfy the preachers by allowing everyone to speak.

2

Invention by Malayalee Diaspora

North American Malayalees have invented some new techniques to be in the limelight. They have formed associations named after their birthplaces in Kerala. (If they displayed this much ingenuity, they could have made a fly swatter, back scratcher stick, and strainer to filter boiling rice 150 years ago.) So, in every Metropolitan city in America, you can see the Kottayam Association, Ranni Association, Tiruvalla Association, Pathanamthitta District Association and so on. They choose a president, two vice-presidents, a secretary, and two joint secretaries, one treasurer, and two joint treasurers, and a coordinator. Most of the attendees will have some titles. Then they send an elaborate report to the Malayalam news media. When the news media receives a good amount of money, they publish the report. Also, these associations would arrange receptions for all the visiting dignitaries from Kerala. Many legislative members, ministers, literary figures, movie actors, judges, religious leaders such as Bishops, pastors, and pulpit preachers, District Collectors, etc.

frequently visit North America. Malayalee ego is a boon for visiting dignitaries because they are accommodated in various homes, and they have an opportunity to visit tourists' locations etc. They receive royal treatment and many visiting persons are offered free shopping opportunities. Finally, local leaders boast about their luck of hosting a bishop, minister, or a movie actor. Usually, most of the Indians are misers, however, they will spend money lavishly for approval and name recognition. At the same time, most of the larger Kerala conventions conduct various humanitarian activities in major cities in Kerala. In those meetings the American dollar would enable them to invite guests starting from State Governor to Panchayat Presidents. The first Malayalee convention of North America was named FOKANA meaning Federation of Kerala Associations in North America. The organization was formed in 1983. It was formed to promote the rich culture and heritage of Kerala, and to stand for the causes of NRIs. FOKANA has become a household name of all Malayalees throughout the world. Most Malayalees, irrespective of cast and creed, desire for their prominence created a   great quarrel, and the leaders went to American court. Subsequently, the opposing faction formed a rival organization called FOMAA, means Federation of Malayalee Associations of Americas. The FOMAA website states that FOMAA is the world's largest overseas Kerala / Malayalee Umbrella organization.

(Kerala, the vibrant state known as "God's own Country" is the Southernmost State of India. Kerala's primary language is "Malayalam" thus the term Malayalee). Founded in 2008, FOMAA comprises 78 Kerala / Malayalee associations throughout North America and Canada. In addition, there is another organization called "World Malayalee "Organization, which has chapters in major cities in America. That organization also split into two many years ago. The same leaders have formed another organization called "India Press club of North America." It has local chapter all over North America. The majority of North American Malayalees are rich, and when it comes to power, position, and prestige they are lavish in giving.

Vacant Houses in Kerala

According to a 2011 Government of India Census, there are 1.19 million houses vacant in tiny Kerala. Millions of Kerala emigrants work in the Middle East, but they cannot become citizens there, hence building a house for them is justified. However, North American Malayalees do not have that problem. In my study, after half a century in America, very few families have gone back to Kerala for retirement life. Some have returned to America after facing weekly strikes, Bandh, and difficulties obtaining simple things from government institutions. Some Malayalees want to return to

America, however, their health and other problems prevent their return to North America. Why do most North American Malayalees build mansions in Kerala especially in rural areas, although they visit there only a few weeks every two or three years? I figured out the psychology behind those activities.

In the past, only five percent of the upper class were affluent in Kerala. Around 20 percent of the population had an average lifestyle. However, the rest of the population lived in abject poverty. However, Poverty and sufferings did not paralyze the population. Christian revivals and education gave great hope and courage for the people. They wanted to excel and conquer the world. The parents sent their children to universities, and then they went to different parts of the world and began to be prosperous. Some of them wanted to display their newfound wealth to the whole community. How do they show it? The best way was to build big mansions, although they did not live there. Many large homes were only inhabited by aging parents, and after their death the house would become vacant. The children who are born in North America have no interest in spending six months to one year in Kerala in order to dispose of their parent's homes or claim their bank accounts. In North America, all business transactions are done without much hassle. In India, to process a transaction is like an expedition to the moon. Hence the bank deposits, gold, and ornaments in safe deposits, along with real estate are abandoned.

Looking back 50 years ago, I can see another reason the Malayalees in North America built big homes in Kerala. Although came as immigrants, only a few wanted to assimilate into the American way of life. Only a tiny percent of the Malayalees like myself understood that we immigrants and our descendants would be permanent in America. Most of them wanted to go back to Kerala after making enough money. However, they did not have the future practical vision about their future lives in America. When the children grew up, they had to face the fact that going back to Kerala is impossible. Most children do not want to live under the barbaric system in Kerala with strikes, Hartal, and Bandh. Hence most Malayalees mindsets were like a "sojourner." Now, most of them have properties in India and they face great difficulties in selling their properties. Due to new regulations and changed economic circumstances, buying and selling are harder now. Many Malayalees who are in their late sixties and seventies are frantically trying to sell their properties. Eventually, many will not be able to sell them.

Leadership Seminars

Many Indian Churches in India and abroad conduct regular special leadership seminars. However, I have never heard of a seminar about "servanthood." How can you become a selfless servant for Jesus?

When I came to Houston fifty years ago, there were five non-Indian Brethren Assemblies in Houston. There are still only five non-Indian assemblies, even after fifty years. The first Indian Brethren Assembly was organized under my leadership, and the first meeting was held in my home in 1975, there were only two Malayalam Assemblies in America besides this assembly in Houston. Other assemblies were in New York and Dallas. At one time there were nine Malayalam Assemblies in Houston. Some assemblies had only three families and eventually they had to close. Today, we have seven Malayalam Brethren Assemblies in Houston. Also, my friend, a Pentecostal pastor, started an Indian Pentecostal Church at the same time. Eventually it multiplied up to 25 Malayalam splinter groups. Today, Houston has more than one dozen Malayalee Pentecostal churches. No Malayalee wants to submit to the authorities. However, when they see a White man, they respect him and they become bootlickers of White men. Most Indians hate White men, and they despise Blacks. However, when they interact with Whites, they will not display hooliganism. I do not consider the White race is more racist than other races. However, all other races display some subtle respect to the White race.

The latest proof is the killing of Tyre Nichols, a Black man in Memphis on January 7, 2023, by five Black police officers. The police stopped him for reckless driving. The officers say that Tyre Nichols ran away. The five Police officers beat this young Black man to a pulp, and he died in the hospital after three days. All these five officers were quickly fired, arrested, and charged with murder. Five Black policemen kill a Black man, and the leftists immediately insists it is "racism" at work. Here the police officers are Black, the police chief and the mayor are Black. For the last 50 years the leftists in America have overseen the universities, media, and corporations. If a systemic racism still prevails, how can you blame the White race. My question is why the mayor and the police chief did not retrain the police to be more humane. If a child kills a neighbor, you cannot blame the White race. I blame the parents.

Here the right question to ask is "Would the Memphis officers have behaved as they did if the man, they were pursing had been White? Upon my research of 40 years, confirm my evaluation about race relations. Unknowingly, most White people have a feeling of superiority, and other races display a subservient behavior to them. Another example is who is leading the riot and looting under the Black Lives Matter Movement. We can see young White males and females are leading the riot. This confirms my study regarding Malayalam Churches and Anglo Churches in America.

There was a Kerala Hindu Society which formed around 40 years ago in Houston. However, they are not above conflicts and divisions. Now each group has subgroups like Christian Churches. Notably in Houston we had many Anglo Pentecostal Churches, however, they never multiplied like the India Pentecostal Church groups.

There is a belief that there are no factional fights in the Episcopal Churches similar to the ones in the Roman Catholic and Orthodox churches. However, the incident in Kerala on Christmas Eve in 2022 erased that misunderstanding. This quote came from the Manorama News: "Ernakulam: Unruly scenes were witnessed inside the St. Mary's Cathedral Basilica here on Friday over the festering row over unified mass."

"Times of India report: KOCHI: *KOCHI: Row over the implementation of the unified format of*"

Those who want to see the violent physical clashes between two groups of priests and their supporters can go to YouTube and watch it. This incident may never happen in a Western Catholic Church.

In 1965, the Kerala Congress was formed. I was one of the five pioneers of the student wing of the Kerala Congress. Later, the Kerala Congress began to split and now there are many groups. In the Congress party alone, there are multiple groups. The same thing is true with the Marxist and other parties. There is a saying in Malayalam about the Kerala Congress, "Kerala Congress grows by splitting and splits again while growing." This is a Malayalee syndrome irrespective of religion or caste.

The Demise of St. Thomas Christians

Most Christians believe that St. Thomas came to Kerala in A.D.52. Whether it is true or not, secular history shows that Christians were in India even in the first century. Then, why are Christians below 3 percent of the Indian population? Although Christianity came to North and South America around 500 years ago, the two continents came under the Christian umbrella. This writer figured out the main reason for the lack of growth of

Christianity in India. I just want to put it in one sentence, "Most Indians do not know how to preach the gospel." A particular behavior is ingrained in our Indian DNA. In preaching and conversation, the majority of Indians insult and attack the opponent with denigrating names. This behavior is displayed in all aspects of Indian life. Even today this is happening in social media. (Clubhouse, YouTube, Facebook, and Instagram) Roman Catholics and Protestants debate daily. Most speakers insult and attack their opponent. There are approximately 1.2 billion Catholics and 800 million Protestants in the world. It is foolish to believe that if they insult each other, they can convert the opponent. I believe that both groups are playing into the hands of the devil. The Eastern Christians, especially the Indian Christians, falsely believe that they are the only true Christians and that Western Christianity is not genuine. Even the great venerated evangelist of India, Sadhu Sunder Singh made similar statements in his speeches in the 1920s. Nowadays, a prominent Telugu brethren scholar who lives in London makes frequent social media posts. According to him, true Christianity is hidden from the Westerners and only an Eastern Christian who is well versed in Hebrew language can comprehend the Bible.

3

The Upper-Caste Hindus Looted the Indian People

Most Indians say that the British looted India. However, their arguments are one-sided. Doing business and making a profit are like "looting" for an Indian. Yes, the British, like other colonial masters, went to India to make money. Most Indians forget the benefits of the British rule by providing education, transportation, and industries. Above all, the removal of slavery, and emancipating women and low caste people are ignored completely. In October 25,2022 an Indian origin, Rishi Sunak became the British Prime Minister. It shows the true humanity of the Capitalist West. Many Indians boast about it; however, can such things happen in tribal and racist India? South Indians have been discriminated against for decades by North Indians. The education system in India is so biased, and from the fourth grade they are taught to hate the West and the White race. They highlight the atrocities of the British and at the same time whitewash the Islamic atrocities and looting of India. They do not want to antagonize the violent Islamic population and try to appease them. Here I am providing some historical facts about the real looters of the people of India.

(Before the Partition of India in 1947, about 584 princely states existed in India, which were not fully and formally part of British India. They were parts of the Indian subcontinent which had not been conquered or annexed by the British, but were under indirect rule and subject to subsidiary alliances. All these kings looted 90 percent of the population, so the upper caste people could lead an affluent lifestyle. Kings of the time ensured the subjugation of the lower caste by imposing heavy taxes on poor people. Besides the taxes on land and crops, peasants had to pay taxes for the right to wear jewelry, the right of men to grow a moustache and even the right of women to cover their breasts. The three upper castes had tax exempt status. The low caste people had to use denigrating or self-depreciating language for conversation. So, the high caste imposed a different dialect for them. If they used the words used by the high caste, they could be killed. They had to substitute words for home, meal, rice, salt etc. Many lower caste people had been murdered for using wrong words. So, who looted India?)

Religious Sermons

You don't need any superior brain to figure this out. It is a matter of common sense. God has given all humans self-worth, and everyone thinks that they are right. Hindus and Muslims also believe that their faith is superior. I remember an incident in my childhood in Ezhumattoor village my birth pace. At that time, Hindus were the majority there. There were only two churches. One was the brethren and the other was a MarThoma Church. Christians were very few in numbers. One Sunday, our Assembly decided to conduct an open-air meeting in Ezhumattoor Junction. We had a visiting evangelist on that Sunday. All church members started a procession singing songs, accompanied with drums and other musical instruments. The loud singing and drums attracted many toward the Junction. Although, I was just in middle school I participated in that procession. When we reached the Junction, the Hindu owner of a coffee shop bestowed hospitality and allowed many to sit on his benches and was very friendly. The crowd also was friendly and welcoming because everyone knew each other. What was the topic of the public speech? It was from Psalms 135:15-18:

15 "the idols of the nations are silver and gold,

the work of human hands.

16 They have mouths, but do not speak;

they have eyes, but do not see;

17 they have ears, but do not hear,

nor is there any breath in their mouths.

18 Those who make them become like them, so do all who trust in them."

Even as a child I was shocked to hear that message. I knew that offensive message was inappropriate. The Psalmist did not pen it for a public gospel meeting. Insulting and making Hindus feel foolish did not attract anyone to Christianity, instead it offended them. 1 Peter 3:15 says, "But sanctify Christ as Lord in your hearts, always being ready to make a defense to everyone who asks you to give an account for the hope that is in you, but with gentleness and respect."

Superiority Syndrome

The basic human behavior all over the world is the same. However, based on power, money, and Socialism, the behavior of many differs in various parts of the world. Upper class Kerala people in a subtle way perfected the art of superiority behavior. Politicians practice it daily. Movie actors in Tamil Nadu cultivated it. When people began to worship some movie actors, politicians, and religious leaders it became a practice, and every generation perpetually follows it. Tamil movie actors M. G. Ramachandran and Sivaji Ganesan were two prime examples. People in a particular city used to organize a reception for him. They would decide a date and time in advance and the news would be published many weeks before hand. Almost one million people would come from far and near. Some devotees would come many days before the event. If the event is scheduled at 10 AM on a particular day, usually the movie actor would arrive only around 6 PM. Still people had no complaints. Politicians also arrive two or three hours late.

In America, Malayalees have associations and churches in major cities. To get publicity and popularity, they organize receptions for ministers and legislators from India. Even communist leaders come to America for medical treatment and to raise money for various projects. The Communist party has been spewing Socialist venom in Kerala for decades. They have been calling America as blood thirsty Capitalists, Colonialists, Revisionists, and many other names. However, instead of going Socialist Paradise like China, Cuba, and the former Soviet Union, they are still coming to America. The local Malayalee groups organize receptions for them and take photos with them. Then they publish this news in newspapers and televisions in Kerala. Some cities in America have elected Malayalees as city Mayors or some other positions. Usually, various Malayalee groups organize some events and invite these local Malayalee leaders as chief guests. It can be Kerala celebrations such as Christmas or Onam. Also, it may be a reception for a leader from Kerala or a book release function. If the reception is advertised at 5.00 PM, no Indians would come on time. It may start around 5:30 PM with an apology for the delay, and a leader who is an expert in Malayalee crowd psychology would come around 5:45 PM. As soon as the leader's responsibility to speak or inaugurate is over he would leave the function in a hurry. The moderator would announce that the chief guest had to leave for another assignment and we were fortunate to get him for our function. Do you know what is really happening? It is a common pattern for leaders and even some evangelists. These leaders in America leave the meeting after their assignment and they go straight to their homes and relax in personal activities or even take a nap. They know the crowd psychology. When a leader is very busy and not available to chit chat with other common people, most people surround the leader and force a conversation. The leader wants to project the image that he is in high demand and relish in his own mind the presumed high stature and respect in the community. There are a few exceptions, however. I remember an event in the nineties. I was invited as a chief guest to a Malayalee Association's annual event in a major Metropolitan city in America. The whole Malayalee community came irrespective of religion since it was a Kerala celebration. After the main event, the organizers arranged a musical event of Malayalam classical songs. Unlike other leaders, I attended the whole musical event. The whole choir group was elated because the chief guest attended their function. I do not consider myself superior to anyone and I view everyone special in their own life because everyone has been created in the image of God; although that image had been marred by sin.

Behavior of Malayalees from the Rest of the Indian People.

The unique Malayalee behavior is a sociological and psychological riddle. A lot of research is necessary to unravel this mystery.

I came to know the different behavior patterns when I went to a University in North India for a master's degree in Economics and a Law degree. Usually in North India you have easy access to government officials or anyone in high positions. It was a pleasant surprise for me. If you go to a doctor's office you can freely talk to the doctor and ask questions and request for a particular test without any fear. I happened to talk to one of my nieces in Kerala on January, 12-2023. Her husband passed away two weeks ago, and she had been suffering from a severe cough and chest discomfort. She went to the only Brethren Hospital in Kerala. Since she had frequent chest discomfort she asked for a cardiologist. The doctor told her that she did not need to see a cardiologist. The doctor did not even order a chest x ray. I asked her how come she did not ask for a chest x ray. She told me that asking the doctor for an x ray, or something is unthinkable for her. She added it may be easier to talk to a Hindu government official without fear. Half a century ago I had to deal with the extreme arrogance of most Kerala doctors. I thought that these barbaric behaviors might have changed. For most Malayalee Christians, a medical doctor is next to Jesus Christ.

In my childhood, I remember that patients and nurses used to call a doctor "Master." Still, most of them behave like a master. Just study the history of Malayalee migrants in North America. Many parents pushed their children to become doctors. More than serving people and the Lord, most of them considered becoming a doctor as a status symbol. Many parents had a below average education and status and they had been poor in India, hence they wanted to obtain family status for the future generations. Now if you go to Kerala, you can see many incompetent doctors. In the past only highly, intelligent students got admission into medical school. Within the last three decades situations have changed. With foreign money, affluent parents donate a high amount of cash to institutions and their children get admissions. The above average student passes the medical exam and becomes a doctor.

Even a porter in a public bus in Kerala shows extreme rude behavior and push people around. A peon in a government office shows more arrogance than his boss. However, people in other parts of India behave differently, especially poor workers who show extra respect to others. There are some Malayalees in high positions in North America, Europe, and Australia. When they travel to India the custom officials and other bureaucrats treat them without any courtesy and dehumanize them. I have read horror stories from many travelers. The situation has improved somewhat now; however, they are not up to the behavioral standards of other Indian people. There is another baffling system among low caste people. There are many untouchables and low caste people. They also maintain a hierarchical racist policy. For example, I am providing an example for two groups. There is a Pulaya caste in Kerala. Below them is another caste called "Pariah" This word is used in English all over the world. They are rejected and despised. Once the world considered North Korea and Libya as Pariah states. Once Pulayas also kept away from the Pariah. Eating food together and intermarriages were prohibited. So, the low caste people suffered, although they were not morally superior than high caste people.

When I discussed this issue with a brother SamKutty Abraham, in our assembly, he provided great insight and explained the root cause. I am thoroughly convinced that his explanation is the correct one.

Kerala was comprised of three kingdoms, Travancore, Cochin, and Malabar. The British was the suzerain of Travancore and Cochin. The local king had complete autonomy, and the   British had only indirect control. There were British residents in Cochin and Travancore. Extreme caste and racial prejudices were maintained in Kerala. When Colonel Munroe was appointed by the queen of Travancore and later King of Cochin as Diwan or de facto ruler, he abolished slavery and many inhuman practices.

However, in other parts of India the British had direct rule and some good Western culture permeated in the society unknowingly. People in North India treat others with dignity, provide good customer service, and equality. A different culture evolved in the North Indian society. However, all North Indians are not angels. Daily many kill Christians and burn churches. Even recently African Black students were beaten up in many cities in India, Dark skin is a curse in Indian society. To support this point, I am here providing some historical evidences. In Houston we have an organization called Kerala Writers Forum. This forum was established to encourage the writers from Kerala. Around two decades ago one member asked a question about Indian Diaspora in South America and the African continent. The Indian community is very prominent throughout Africa, and they controlled the whole economy. However, you did not find a single family from Kerala in those areas before 1950s. Nobody had the answer, but I provided the answer. The British had no direct control of the Kerala population. The British, by force, brought other Indians to Africa and South America as laborers in plantations and other fields. Millions of people were brought in in the eighteenth and nineteenth centuries. Yes, Malayalees can be found in every nook and corner of the world. Since the 1950s, they voluntarily migrated to other countries to support their families. This is the reason we do not see any major Kerala population in South America and the African continent.

Indentured Labor: Forced Migration into Africa

"The second wave of migration into Africa by Indians came because of colonization. Major clusters of Indians were taken as indentured labors across colonial empires in the nineteenth and early twentieth century. Indentured Indian laborers replaced freed slaves in plantation economies. The stark contrast between the first trade wave was that migration during Colonial rule was forced, not voluntary. It is worth noting that some Indians migrated as clerks and teachers to serve colonial governments overseas. This expanded colonial rule. Estimates during the period of 1829-1924 suggest that about 769,427 Indians migrated out of India into Mauritius, South Africa, Seychelles, and the East African region.

During colonization, the sub-continent India and large masses of Africa were incorporated into the British Empire, such as Sierra Leone and the most common example, South Africa. Indentured labor came as the result of the bondage of debt. Through this, European imperialists facilitated the transport of over 3.5 million Indians into the African continents where they served as labor for plantations. A majority of these plantations grew sugar. Unlike indentured laborers before 1830, most indentured laborers post-1830 did not return into free labor markets. They were forced to renew contracts.

Even as numerous sources account for the inhumane conditions of laborers, the populations only grew. In Mauritius 1871, the Indian population doubled from 33% in 1846 to 66% of the total population within the state. Migration remained predominantly male until the mid-nineteenth century. States then started to encourage the forced migration of women, to meet growing demands for domestic, urban and plantation labor, and create a consistent population of indentured slaves directly into their economy."

South Africa

During the Colonial Era, Indians were accorded the same subordinate status in South African society as Blacks were by the W, which held the vast majority of political power. During the period of Apartheid from 1948 to 1994, Indian South Africans were called and often voluntarily accepted, terms which ranged from "Asians" to "Indians", and were legally classified as being members of a single racial group. Some Indian South Africans believed that these terms were improvements on the negatively defined identity of "Non-White", which was their previous status. Politically conscious and nationalistic Indian South Africans wanted to show both their heritage and their local roots in South Africa. Increasingly they self-identified as "African", "South African" and when necessary, "Indian South

Africans".] During the most intense period of segregation and apartheid, "Indian", "Asian", "Colored" and "Malay" group identities controlled numerous aspects of daily life, including where a classified person was permitted to live and study.

The "Indian" racial identity was created by both internal political movements that sought to consolidate support amongst the different Indian ethnicities in the face of discrimination; and the Apartheid government which strictly codified the physical and cultural boundaries between "race groups", and encouraged these group identities.[7] As a result of these Apartheid rules, South Africans continue to identify themselves, and informally classify each other as, "Blacks ", "whites", "Colored" and "Indians". Despite having a presence in South Africa for more than 150 years and being an officially recognized part of the population since 1961, Indians are still sometimes viewed as a foreign presence in the country, and find themselves having to justify their belonging to South Africa as a homeland". The above history proves that the Malayalees were immune from forced migration.

Adulterated Food

Adulterated food is a national problem and may be more prevalent in Kerala recently.

I remember while growing up in Kerala, eating cooked rice had been stressful and   fearful. While chewing rice, stones would damage the teeth.

The main food in Kerala is rice. It is unavoidable if you live there. Most people in Kerala had been frustrated and cursed the merchants. However, they had no clue how this problem started. In many places the merchants in Kerala, Tamil Nadu, and Andhra Pradesh purposely mixed special sands with rice to make profits. Since India is not a free-market economy the oligarchs could do whatever, they wanted. Hence in the past merchants kept bags of sand and mixed it before selling. In America we buy brown rice from Indian stores. Outside the bag is printed "Export quality no stones." Recently, I haven't seen the advertisement of stones. "This evil system had been transferred to the future generation and the new generation found novel methods and extended the malpractice for all food products.

BBC Report January 9, 2023

"The owner and chief cook of an eatery in the southern Indian state of Kerala have been arrested in connection with the death of a customer allegedly due to food poisoning.

A nurse who worked in the Kottayam district had ordered the food online.

Police said 21 others also fell ill after eating food from the eatery.

Police have invoked charges of culpable homicide against the owner and the cook. They are in custody and have not yet commented on the allegations.

The incident is among a spate of food poisoning cases in the state that have led to concerns about the safety of restaurant food.

Rashmi Raj, a nurse at the Kottayam Medical College, was admitted to hospital on December 30 , 2022 after falling ill from eating a rice dish and barbecued chicken that she had ordered from the eatery. She succumbed to her illness on January, 2, 2023.

According to local news reports, a preliminary post-mortem indicated she had died due to an infection in her internal organs.

Several others who ate food from the same restaurant also reported ill. Police say their investigation has confirmed food poisoning as the cause of the nurse's death and that the quality of food served at the restaurant was "poor."

Food poisoning cases were also reported in other parts of the state last week. In the Pathanamthitta district, several students and parents fell ill after eating food served at a school event. In the same district, nearly 100 people fell sick after eating food served at a baptism. Since then, food safety officials have raided over 500 eateries across the state. Forty-eight eateries have been suspended for operating in unsanitary conditions or without a proper license.

Officials say the inspections are expected to continue.

Similar raids had been conducted in May 2022 when a 16-year-old died and several others fell sick after eating at a snack bar in the Kasaragod district".

5 Most Common Adulterated Foods in India

June 26, 2020 Khushbu Singh

What is food adulteration?

Motivated by economic profitability or malicious intent, adding or mixing substandard or harmful substances to food items that may have adverse effect on health is known as food adulteration. The most common adulterated foods in India include:

Milk – India is the world's largest producer and consumer of milk and related products. Unfortunately, it has become notoriously infamous for being the country to produce synthetic/artificial milk. Driven by increased urbanization, high demand and unethical profit motives, adulteration and contamination of milk has become a serious problem. Contaminants range from water to chemicals such as caustic soda, white paint, refined oil, urea, starch, glucose, and formalin. Detergent is often detected due to lack of hygiene in handling and packaging. Either way the health risks of the resulting mixture is very high. The World Health Organization (WHO) recently issued an advisory to the Government of India. It states that if milk and related products adulteration was not checked immediately, then by 2025, 87 per cent of its citizens may suffer from serious diseases like cancer.

Milk products – Just as gloomy is the situation with milk products such as paneer, ghee, yoghurt, butter and cream. Paneer is a staple for vegetarians in the country. In the market, it is often replaced with synthetic paneer which is made from a mixture of maida, palm oil, baking powder, detergent, bicarbonate soda, skimmed milk and sulphuric acid. Similarly, synthetic butter, yogurt and cream replacements are manufactured from a combination of chemicals and oils. The 'real' ghee has been replaced by butter oil. A wide variety of Indian sweets available are made from adulterated milk and milk products posing risks for human health.

Tea/Coffee - Tea and coffee are the most consumed beverages In India. If your idea of a perfect evening is enjoying a hot cup of tea, then you need to know that adulteration of tea has taken place since the early 1800s. To enhance the aroma and taste, the tea leaves are mixed with artificial food color, flavors, and synthetic dye such as tartrazine, indigo, gypsum, graphite, and Prussian blue. Coffee is ubiquitous food product of considerable economic value. It is often mixed with cheaper materials like clay powder, corn powder, chicory, woody tissues etc. to increase profitability.

Honey - In ancient times, honey was 'elixir of life'. However, in 2020 this definition for commercially available honey does not hold much ground. In the year 2010 and 2016, CSE and Consumer Voice respectively conducted tests on popular honey brands available in India. In both instances, they detected rampant use of adulterants and antibiotics. Artificial honey is manufactured in illegal factories using sugar, corn, or rice syrup to cater to rising demand. Artificial honey is devoid of trace minerals present in natural honey and therefore causes more harm than good to human health. Additionally, at an alarming rate honeybees are being given antibiotics to keep them disease free. Besides, farmers often spray chemical pesticides on crops and flora to protect their yield. The Bees while foraging on nectar consume the deadly spray. The Bees exposure to antibiotics and pesticides ultimately adulterates honey.

'Masala' Powders - Spices and herbs are labor-intensive to produce, which keeps their prices high compared to other crops. Indian kitchens use a variety of spices such as cardamom, clove, nutmeg, peppercorns, and cumin. Growing demand, production challenges and high prices make spices particularly tempting targets for food adulterators. To enhance the aroma, color and texture of spices, different types of cheap chemicals are used. For instance, 'Sudan 1' a red dye also a known carcinogen, is used to cater red color to chilly powders. Similarly, adulterant like lead chromate is used to impart bright yellow color to turmeric. Also, to increase the weight of the spice packaging cheap fillers are used. For example, a packaged garam masala may contain saw dust or powdered bran while a pack of saffron may contain colored maize thread."

If India adopted free market system instead of Socialism this problem would not have occurred. Government control regulation stifles the market.

Untouchability In INDIA Is The Worst Form Of Slavery

I am providing a brief history of untouchability in Kerala to prove my arguments about the extreme racism and arrogance in Kerala society.

Untouchability originated from the ancient Hindu religion and social systems. According to the Traditional Hindu "Varna" system a person is born into one of the four castes based on Karma and purity. Those born as Brahmans are priests and teachers, Kshatriyas are rulers and soldiers, Vaishyas are merchants and traders, and Sudras are laborers. Untouchables are literally outcastes. They are not included in any of the traditional Varna or caste system of the Hindu religion. According to Dr. Ambedkar, untouchables form an entirely new class i.e., the fifth Varna apart from the existing four castes. Around 200 million people in India are considered "untouchable"- people tainted by their birth into a caste system that deems them impure and less than human. Once these untouchables were not allowed to drink from the same well, attend the same temples, wear shoes in the presence of an upper caste Hindu or drink from the same cups. They are relegated to the lowest jobs and lived in constant fear of being publicly humiliated, paraded naked, and beaten and raped with impunity by upper caste Hindus seeking to keep them in their place. Merely walking through an upper caste neighborhood was a life-threatening offence. Even though untouchability was officially banned when India adopted its constitution in 1950, discrimination against the low caste remained so pervasive that in 1989 the Government passed the legislation known as "The Prevention of Atrocities Act 1989." The Act specifically made it illegal to parade people naked through the streets, force them to eat feces, take away their land, foul their water, and burn down their homes, and interfere with their right to vote. In rural India, the above-mentioned incidents happen even today.

The people of Kerala in South India practiced the worst form of untouchability in the world. Swami Vivekananda a Hindu sage, reformer, and philosopher called Kerala a "lunatic asylum." This quote is from Vivekananda's work "The Future of India," "Was there ever a sillier thing before in the world than what I saw in Malabar country? The poor Pariah is not allowed to pass through the same streets as the high cast man, but if he changes his name to a hodge-podge English name it is alright, or to a Mohammedan name. It is alright. What inference would you draw except that these

Malabaris are all lunatics, their homes so many lunatic asylums."

A Nair (a middle-class caste) could behead a low caste person if he touched him, and a similar fate awaited a slave who did not turn out off the road as the Nair passed. According to Kerala tradition, low caste people were forced to maintain 64 feet from high caste people, as they were thought to pollute them. Based on caste hierarchy, some were to keep distances of 72 feet, 32 feet, and 24 feet respectively. Even in the beginning of the twentieth century, the high caste men, when walking along the road, uttered a warning grunt or hoot to people of lower caste to keep enough distance. Lower caste people had no right to tile their house, to build an upstairs building, or a gateway. No man could approach him with more than a single cloth around his waist which should not fall below his knees. If a man of lower caste were by misfortune to touch a Nair lady, her relatives would immediately kill her and the man who touched her and all his relatives. Low caste people when speaking expected to cover their mouth, using in conversation a self-depreciating form of speech with special standardized servile expressions and submissive bodily postures.

The British Outlawed Most of the Outrageous Practices

Breast Tax (MULAKKARAM)

This is the story of a low caste Hindu woman who lived in the 19th century in a place called "Cherthala" in Kerala, South India. The state government had imposed a breast tax on low caste Hindu women called "Mulakkaram" (Breast Tax) which was to be paid so that they could cover their breasts. The tax rate was determined based on the size of the breast. Upper caste women could cover their breasts without paying any tax. In 2012, Kerala observed the 200th anniversary of the end of the breast tax. The following facts are from an article published in "The Hindu" on October 21, 2013, by Nidhi Surendra Nath." Nangeli, who lived in Cherthala in Alappuzha over 200 years ago, gained her place in history as the woman who cut off her breasts to protest against the inhuman Mulakkaram (breast tax) that was imposed in the erstwhile kingdom of Travancore" (Kerala).

Caste Oppression

Kings of the time ensured the subjugation of the lower caste by imposing heavy taxes on them. Their wealth was built on some of the worst taxes imposed anywhere in the world. Besides the tax on land and crops, peasants had to pay taxes for the right to wear jewelry, the right of men to grow a moustache, and even the right of women to cover their breast. (There were a hundred similar silly taxes.) The three upper castes had tax exempt status. Colonel John Munroe removed all taxes for the poor low caste people and taxed all the upper caste people. This invited a great uproar against John Munroe from the upper caste people. The heavy taxes ensured that the lower castes were kept eternally in debt while members of the upper caste flourished. Nangeli was a poor Ezhava woman from Cherthala. Her family could not afford to pay the taxes and was in debt to the rulers. The Tax Collector then called "Pravathiar came to her house to demand the tax because she covered her breasts. Then Nangeli cut off one of her breasts and presented it to the Tax Collector". The Tax Collector fled in fear while Nangeli bled to death at her door step. Her husband, Mr. Kandappan, who was away during the incident, after returning jumped on her funeral pyre and died. The very next day the tax was withdrawn by the Sree Mulam Thirunal, Maharaja of Travancore, fearing public agitation. In Kerala, the British Ruler Colonel Munroe reformed Kerala society.

Now the reader may get some insight because most Kerala people behave in such arrogant ways thinking that they are born leaders.

Religious Functions

Kerala society, irrespective of religion and caste, people follow similar behavioral pattern. In India, if they start a school or construct a bridge, they want to bring the highest official available to inaugurate, if possible, the Governor or Chief Minister. I remember in our village for the golden Jubilee celebration of our middle school, the Chief Minister of Kerala, Pattom A. Thanu Pillai was the chief guest. If there is a Catholic funeral or wedding, they would try to bring the Cardinal or Archbishop to officiate. It is a status function. If it is Orthodox, the chief guest must be Catholicos or Patriarch. In the MarThoma Church they would try to bring the top bishop (Valia Tirumeni). The Marmon Convention is one of the largest conventions in the world. This convention started 128 years ago by the pioneers of the Mar Thoma Church. The tent has a seating capacity in excess of 160,000 people. They are seated on the dry sand bed.

Every year the organizers bring a White Western preacher to bring a higher status for this convention although Kerala has many scholarly preachers. However, there were some exceptions.

Regarding Pentecostals, they would bring the national or state president pastors. In Brethren churches, there are many tiers of preachers. Every Brethren Church is independent, and there are no central organizations or national leaders. Instead, everyone makes a personal evaluation and invites certain preachers. Like others, they also give importance to physical appearance. Preachers who are tall, have light complexion and great oratory skills are in great demand. When more churches invite those speakers, they achieve a cultic status, and everyone wants those speakers. So, the unwritten grading system for preachers starts from one star to seven-star preachers. If a preacher has a dark complexions, and short stature, and if he is a scintillating speaker, he may get some access to pulpits. Sometimes, during annual weeklong conferences and camps, some seven-star preachers stay in their own rooms and never mingle with regular believers. When they meet an acquaintance, they may chit chat for two minutes and leave. However, in America most famous Anglo preachers go around and interact with the young and old alike. If two Indian preachers are scheduled in one event, one preacher may be preparing notes for his next sermon while the other speaker is speaking in a loud voice. Sometimes the loudest speaker may get the highest score. You will not find a superiority complex with most of the Anglo preachers. The seven-star Indian preachers, however, have great and edifying messages. Their sermons are good, if we can follow them. They say all the right things, however, they behave as if it is not applicable to them. I am sure they are not cognizant of their shortcomings. They do not have a blind spot detecting mirror in their brain. Only a self-evaluation can solve the problem with such Christians. Over the years many people called my attention to such preachers. There are a few of them. One time somebody was talking about the egotism of some preachers. One devotee of a great speaker tried to whitewash and stated that he had been very reserved from childhood, and he was not a big talker. Then I told the devotee that his answer is scripturally wrong. I expressed my opinion like this, 2 Corinthians 5:17 says, "This means that anyone who belongs to Christ has become a new person. The old life is gone; a new life has begun!". According to the aforesaid verse and the entire Bible proclaim that we can modify our behavior after the new birth. One of my neighbors was a chain smoker. However, after he was born again, he stopped smoking immediately and he never had a side effect due to sudden cessation of smoking. This incident may be an exception. We all know that if someone is a habitual smoker or alcoholic, they may need a long rehabilitation treatment to recover from their previous habits. If a habitual thief or a habitual liar become believers, we expect honesty from them. If a great preacher still lies, his devotees cannot say that he has been stealing and lying from childhood. Similarly, a reserved person, especially a travelling evangelist must modify his behavior and display humility. At the same time a believer should be careful to avoid unnecessary conversations and too many jokes. I have seen both extreme behaviors in some preachers. You might have figured out what happened to Christianity in India. The Indian Christians must change the method of proclaiming the gospel. Dr Billy Graham is a great role model. He never denounced other religions, instead, he proclaimed the love and sacrifice of Jesus and millions became Christians. There are exceptions to every rule. Good and civilized discussions are fruitful, like the debates between Jerry Thomas and

Zakir Naik, or the one between Poet Laureate K. V. Simon and Krishnan Nambiar, M.A.(Honors).

53

4

Economic Paralysis in Kerala

It was announced that the iPhone 14 will be manufactured in Tamil Nādu starting in September 2022. The Wall Street Journal on March 4,2023, reports by Rajesh Roy, Yoko Kubota and Philip Wen

"Top Apple Supplier Foxconn plans Major India Growth. Apple inc.'s main manufacturer, Foxconn Technology Group, is considering a major expansion in India , including possibly assembling millions more iPhones and setting up new production sites as it seeks to further diversify beyond China. Foxconn is set to expand production of iPhones at its existing plant near Chennai, in the southern Indian state of Tamil Nadu, people familiar with the matter said. It aims to boost iPhone production to around 20 million unis annually by 2024, up from about 6 million, and roughly triple the number of workers to as many as 100,000, and the people, including a senior India government official.

Foxconn also plans to build a new production facility in the southern Karnataka state, where it would make products including iPhones, people familiar with the matter said.

In addition, Foxconn is considering building a new production site, in the southern city of

Hyderabad as well as a silicon carbide fabrication plant and packing facility in India for its semiconductor business, some of the people said."

Have you thought about why no companies start businesses in Kerala? Bangalore is the Silicon Valley of India. Thousands of foreign companies are operating in Karnataka, Tamil Nadu, and Andhra Pradesh. Some Malayalees who had great businesses in America and the Middle East started some businesses in Kerala in the past. They did so with a good heart, but not with a good head. They loved Kerala so much, and they made big investments in Kerala. However, as you know, every other day Kerala politicians or trade unions declare Hartal or Bandh. Also trade union workers demand exorbitant pay and boycott work. Usually, they will stop vehicles, including ambulances, and prevent them from reaching their destinations. Over the years many people have died due to lack of medical care. People who were bitten by snakes died on the way to the hospital since they could not reach the hospital due to violent strikes. Many pregnant women have died as well.

Many Keralites consider business as evil and businesspeople as looters. Consequently, no one dares to start a business in Kerala. You may not know it, but it is true that some Pravasi (Diaspora) Malayalees had to commit suicide due to the labor union persecution. It is interesting to observe that many Malayalees who burned down the buses and cars in Kerala happened to come to America. One of my cousins was a Naxalite (armed Communist fighter) in Kerala and had been in jail. He was a Christian by birth. He and many others like him have come to America, and live like kings, enjoying the fruit of Capitalism. However, they become very productive employees. If the work starts at 8:00 AM, they will arrive at 7.30 AM and work hard to impress their white bosses. No Hartal or picketing! The communist ideology and practices have corrupted many Keralites. However, when they migrated to America, they realized it would not work. Many Malayalees are in Anglo assemblies, and many are elders, too. I am an elder along with two other Malayalees in our assembly. Malayalees do not create any problems in Anglo Assemblies. If they displayed one tenth of the same discipline in Malayalam Assemblies there would not have been seven Malayalam assemblies in Houston. If you study the conditions of the assemblies outside Kerala, you will learn that there are less quarrels and splits. If there are Malayalee brethren, they tend to promote groupism which causes divisions. There will be less splits if the locals are left alone there.

Vizhinjam International Seaport

The Vizhinjam International Deepwater Multipurpose Seaport, also known as the Vizhinjam Port is an under-construction port on the Arabian Sea coast city of Trivandrum, India.

"Most people in Kerala conducted numerous protests to cancel this life changing project.

The idea for a port at Vizhinjam was first mooted by Travancore Diwan Ramaswamy Ayyar. However, the present under-construction port was originally conceived about 25 years ago.

What was the Adani group's Vizhinjam port project?

Then foundation stone of the Rs 7,525 crore port, being built under a Public Private Partnership (PPP) model with Adani Ports Private Limited at Vizhinjam on near Thiruvananthapuram, was laid by then Kerala Chief Minister Oommen Chandy in December 2015. It has since missed its completion deadline.

The port is to have 30 berths, and will be able to handle giant "mega" container ships. The Adani Group has said the ultramodern port, located close to major international shipping routes, will boost India's economy. Its location is also of strategic importance, the project's supporters have claimed. The port is expected to compete with Colombo, Singapore, and Dubai for a share of trans-shipment traffic.

While the fishermen's protests are being supported by the Latin Catholic Church, a local people's action committee is demanding speedy completion of the project. This committee has the backing of various Hindu community outfits like the upper caste Nair Service Society, besides the OBC Hindu organization, like the Sree Narayana Dharma Paripalana Yogam, as well as the Vaikunda Swami Dharma Pracharana, which has a considerable presence among the Nadar community in southern Kerala.

Opponents BJP and CPI(M) have made common cause over the port project, criticizing the protesters.

Senior CPI(M) leader and state education minister V Sivankutty has blamed the Latin Catholic Church, alleging there is a bid to create a riot. Pro-Left media in the state had also alleged involvement of foreign funding behind the fishermen's agitation.

BJP state president K Surendran has said the forces that had organized the protest the Kudankulam nuclear power plant near Kanyakumari in Tamil Nadu, were behind the Vizhinjam protest. The Kudankulam protest was spearheaded by the Latin Catholic diocese of Tuticorin

By Matters India Reporter

Thiruvananthapuram, Nov 28, 2022: The police in Kerala have registered a case against a Catholic archbishop, his auxiliary and 48 others in connection with violence during a protest under construction international seaport in the southern Indian state.

The police and protesters clashed at the Vizhinjam police station close to the port protest site on the night of November 27th, which led to injuries to more than 50 people, including 36 police personnel.

The violent mob also ransacked the police station and destroyed equipment and police vehicles parked in the compound.

The protesters came to the police station demanding the release of five men detained by the police, the previous day for a violent clash in front of the port site. The protestors had blocked the entry of dumpster trucks with construction materials.

Some people claiming to be supporters of the port project, accompanied the trucks and threw stones at the protestors.

The clash continued allegedly in connivance with the police. Many had sustained wounds in the violence.

The police later charged Archbishop Thomas J Nettor of the Trivandrum Latin archdiocese, his auxiliary Bishop R Kristudas, priests, and other protesters for the violence.

Father Eugene Pereira, convener of the protest, blamed the Communist-led Kerala coalition government and the Adani Group that is constructing the multi-billion-dollar seaport project for the violence.

"Archbishop Netto, Bishop Kristudas and many priests and others named in the FIR (First Information Report) were not present at the protest site," Father Pereira told media persons November 28th.

The priest denied any protesters who were indulged in the November 27, 2022, violence at the police station. "It is true our people were there in the police station, but somebody else in the crowd had attacked the station and put the blame on us."

A priest who was wounded in the police action said the police personnel behaved so violently at the protestors. He was hit on the head with a baton.

This protest is not an isolated incident. It has nothing to do with preventing environmental disasters or helping poor fishermen. History would provide adequate reason for this degenerated DNA. In the sixties the Communist party prevented the introduction of tractors and other machinery for modern farming in Kuttanad. The self-proclaimed specialists concluded that modernization would create severe unemployment. In the seventies, they prevented computerization in universities and government offices.

I published my first book in 1994 titled "Capitalism - A Panacea for Socio- Economic Woes." I argued in the book that the large population in India is a boon, although all Indian Economists taught erroneously that overpopulation is the main cause for our maladies. Also, India is very rich in natural resources. We all had to leave Kerala because of Socialism. All Socialist countries are poor. Singapore has no resources, so how did they become affluent? Nehru and Congress followed Socialism. Then in 1991, P V Narasimha Rao liberalized Indian economy which allowed foreign companies to establish in India. Although the liberalization was only 25 percent India made rapid progress. If they had liberalized completely, India could have surpassed America. Why is China the second largest economy? Communism is only for administration. They liberalized economy in 1979 because the Chinese were more farsighted than the Indians. I will be writing an essay on Sir C. P. Ramaswamy Iyer later in this work. His vision was to keep Kerala as a separate country with Capitalism. Today, most Malayalees abroad would still be living in Kerala. Look how Socialism is ingrained in Indian DNA. The best example is the Vizhinjam port protest. The history is repeated. In the sixties, Marxist were against introducing tractors and other machinery in Kuttanad. In the seventies, Communists were against computerization in colleges and government offices. After destroying our generation when Communist leaders came to

America, they understood their foolishness and started private enterprises. When Jyoti Basu visited America, he also had a change of heart. However, he was too old and died. Today, Bengalese are predominantly manual laborers in Kerala. Kerala could have faced the same situation. Kerala avoided it because their people migrated all over the world, and are sending billions of dollars. I usually do not respond to our people. Most Indians brag about the top level of Indians in American corporations. There are two dozen chairmen of Indian origin and about 40 percent of Indian employees in major companies. I agreed with those people. All Indians feel the same way. My message for them is that they should have felt a righteous indignation instead of a false pride. The leaders of these American companies if they were in India, would have become mediocre employees eating peanuts, Vada, and coffee. Their brain did not expand as soon as they landed in an American airport. American capitalism made it possible for Indians to thrive in America, this was my point in the book. Indians are smarter than all other people, however, Socialism robbed their opportunity to thrive.

A Latin bishop is leading the violent protest in Vizhinjam. If that port is finished, it would change the whole state of Kerala. The government has met most of their demands. Then again, they would bring additional demands which means they wanted to stop the construction.

The underlying reason is jealousy and evil in the minds of the Kerala people. The name "Adani" created a violent allergic reaction among the evil Leftists. Adani and Ambani did not loot anyone. They are shrewd businesspeople. Just imagine, if all the private companies were eliminated, our standard of living would revert back one century. Does anyone remember how our telephone system worked before privatization? If I had to make a call from Tiruvalla to Kottayam, I had to call the exchange and book a call. It was called Trunk booking. After a few hours I might get a connection. People don't appreciate the comfort and convenience that Capitalism created. Today, we can make video calls free of charge. Private competition has made it possible. When my mother passed away in 2001. I did not call her frequently because of the exorbitant telephone bill for international calls. Capitalism creates wealth.

When the British introduced an Indian railway system, there were widespread protest all over India. They thought it was a conspiracy of White Colonial masters to drag India to England. The above story may be hard to believe in the twenty-first century.

Automobile

As with any transformative new technology, automobiles encountered considerable resistance when they arrived on the American scene in larger numbers between 1900 and 1910. There's no doubt that they became popular—one of the features of American life at that time was the birth of dozens of automobile enthusiasts' "clubs," a network that quickly coalesced into the American Automobile Association, which was founded in 1902.

European Americans generally relied on oxen and wagons for extended overland travel. Oxen were sturdy and steady. They could pull wagons for longer distances and with less maintenance than that required by horses. Oxen could also be consumed if an injury necessitated euthanasia. Sea travel was arduous, and people usually attempted long voyages only when it was unavoidable. A journey across the Atlantic could take up to eight weeks depending on sailing conditions. Ocean travelers also exposed themselves to many dangers and discomforts, including piracy, drowning, and disease.

Millions of people lost jobs when the automobile was introduced. However, the living standards and comfort and affluence only increased by introducing cars. People in America and Europe also resisted modern inventions such as the automobile, printing press, telephone, cell phone and many other inventions. Now Kerala people are protesting the modern rail system where people can reach their destination faster than today. Travel time can be cut down in half. They also protested the Nedumbassery International Airport in the nineties. In addition, with every project the protesters have the same reasons. Environmental damage and loss of job etc. Today. on December 6, 2022, I read in the media that the 140 days of cantankerous protests by fishermen against the Vizhinjam sea port has been settled. The Adani business group who is building their port stated that they lost 220 crores rupees due to the strike. Now you know why nobody wants to touch business in Kerala. Whatever the companies do to satisfy trade union demands, the next day they come up with another cock and bull story and make further outlandish demands.

5

Universal Brain Malfunction

The fall of Adam and Eve in the garden of Eden corrupted the human brain.

Even after becoming a Christian that corruption still exists. According to 2 Corinthians 5:17, "Therefore, if anyone is in Christ, he is a new creation; old things have passed away; behold, all things have become new."

What about the Christian who continues to sin? There is a difference between continuing to sin and continuing to live in sin. No one reaches sinless perfection in this life, but the redeemed Christian is being sanctified (made holy) day by day, sinning less and hating it more each time he fails. Yes, we still sin, but unwillingly and less and less frequently as we mature. Our new self-hates the sin that still has a hold on us. The difference is that the new creation is no longer a slave to sin, as we formerly were. We are now freed from sin and it no longer has power over us (Romans 6:6-7). Now we are empowered by and for righteousness. We now have the choice to "let sin reign" or to count ourselves "dead to sin but alive to God in Christ Jesus" (Romans 6:11-12). Best of all, now we have the power to choose the latter.

All have different views on social, economic, and political matters. Many people, even many

Christians believe and propagate outlandish propaganda. This is the reason I wrote the book on Conspiracy Theories. That book is available on Amazon. Many Christians in the past have set dates for Jesus's second coming. However, it never happened. Still, they never learned a lesson and foolishly set new dates. In politics, Leftists and Rightists have their own conspiracy theories. When Trump was elected, there was a conspiracy group that came into existence. They are known as QAnon. They had daily broadcasts with so called inside news from the military etc. Many highly qualified Christians also followed and believed them. In 2020, Trump failed to win the presidency. QAnon believed and promoted the idea that Trump would declare Martial Law with the support of the military and would stay in power. On October 28,2017, they stated that Hillary Clinton would be arrested in two days. First, they predicted that Trump will be reinstated on March 4, 2021. Then they changed the date to March 20. Again, they told their supporters that Trump will be reinstated on August 13,2021. The rumors got momentum and it circulated on social media. Two highly qualified international preachers shared this news with me. I had to reply to them harshly and rebuked them for believing such propaganda.

Some believed that Trump was and is still in charge of the Military. They believed it.

Why did I write this example? I want to prove one-point. High intelligence and advanced degrees are no guarantee in the discernment of foolish theories.

Sir C P Ramaswamy Iyer. Diwan, Travancore 1931-1936

For every Malayalee the name Sir C. P. is similar to, the response of the name Hitler to a Jew. From childhood we have heard about atrocities of Sir C. P. from family, friends, school, and society. People don't have the time, or resources and intellectual acumen to verify the veracity of all stories. All historians write history with their bias. After September 11, 2001, with the bombings of twin Towers and killing of thousands of innocent people, the Islamic world provided a different narration. Many people in the Islamic world celebrated the tragic deaths. According to many Muslims, Bin Ladin was a freedom fighter who was fighting against Western Imperialism. However, most people in the civilized world saw him as a terrorist. As Christians, the Bible instructs them to be good citizens and obey the laws of the land as long as the law doesn't go against Christian principles. In the same way most Kerala people believe that the rebellion in 1921 in Kerala called "Mappila Lahala" was a freedom struggle. That revolt was the forerunner of the ISIS massacres in the Middle East.

After the Second World War at Nuremberg, Germany, many high-ranking Nazi leaders were hanged, and many went to jail for a long time. They were charged for crimes against humanity by the International Tribunal. In India also, a British commander committed atrocities and killed hundreds of innocent people in Amritsar, Punjab. It was known as the Jallianwala Bagh massacre. Brigadier General R.E. H. Dyer was responsible for this atrocity. The army was retrained and developed less violent tactics for crowd control. The attack was condemned by the Secretary of State, Winston Churchill, as "Utterly Monstrous" and the U.K. House of Commons debated on July 8,1920. The members of Parliament voted 247 to 37 against Dyer and he was removed from his position.

Why have I written about this historical event? If Sir C.P. was like Hitler, how he was appointed by Nehru and others in high positions in India? Kerala lost a great visionary. There was a mass hysteria against C.P, and the Communists exploited the situation. The Congress party and others became sympathizers of the violent seditious revolt in Punnapra Vylar. In Kerala, somehow low caste people believe that the Communists were their saviors. They believe that other parties stand for rich people. This is a universal symptom. In America, also, 99 percent of Blacks, and people from third world countries especially from India support the Democratic Party. Any ruler in the world would have done exactly what C. P did in such situations.

He suppressed the violent takeover of a large portion of the state by the Communists. His idea was to establish an American model democracy for Kerala. When they heard American model, they lost all their sanity, similar to hearing the Adani and Ambani name for the present Kerala population. Envy is a basic human trait. However, one can see its highest form from the people of India. Russians, Chinese and people from all over the world come to the USA. They love and adore and love America. However, if you conduct a conversation with an Indian in America, you can hear virulent stories against the White man and the American system.

If Kerala became an independent country, it would have become like Singapore, South Korea, or Japan within two decades and none of us would had have to leave Kerala. These are hypothetical scenarios and now the situation is different. Was Sir C.P racist? Yes, he was racist like all the politicians in Kerala from the past to the present. This writeup may create great hatred and opposition. I understand the risks. A quarter of a century ago, I had to write another revolutionary piece like this. All Malayalees take great pride in V. K. Krishna Menon, who was a defense minister in Nehru's cabinet. All Malayalees proudly say that Krishna Menon spoke 9 hours continuously in the United Nations General Assembly in New York. Since India was in the orbit of the Soviet Union it supported India. His speech for more than eight hours never convinced a single nation to change their view on Kashmir. It is interesting to note the longest speeches made in the United Nations. African and other Socialist leaders took an opportunity to blame the West and Capitalism for their misfortunes. We all know that long speeches are a disgrace for a society. The human brain has the capacity to listen for the first 30 minutes, after that, people will be listening less. If the speech is eloquent and scintillating, people may listen for one hour. Who in the world has time to sit and listen to political babbling for hours? The greatest evangelist, Billy Graham who spoke more than anyone in the world spoke around 30 minutes and millions of people accepted Jesus Christ as their personal Savior. The great Communicator Ronald Regan mesmerized people with 30-minute speeches. Most people boast in irrelevant and foolish things. Krishna Menon was a staunch Socialist and Anti-American racist. As Defense Minister he was a great failure. Although India spent a lot of money for defense when the Chinese attacked India in 1962, they easily defeated India. President Kennedy had to send emergency weapons to save India and Krishna Menon had to resign in disgrace. So, my point is that humans tend to demonize or deify some people based on a propaganda.

From Wikipedia, the free encyclopedia

Sir C.P wanted to construct a mega port in Vizhinjam. He founded most industries of Kerala.

Most people of Kerala are not aware of the greatest industrial base he established.

Sir Chetput Pattabhiraman Ramaswamy Iyer 1879-1966. He was popularly known as Sir C.P. was an Indian lawyer, administrator, and politician who served as the Advocate- General of the Madras presidency from 1920- to 1923, In addition, he was a law member of the Executive Council of the Viceroy of India from 1931to 1936 and the Diwan of Travancore from 1936 to 1947.

He wanted to link the Vizhinjam port to the Vellayani Lake with a channel. Widespread opposition arose from all corners of Kerala at that time.

C. P. Ramaswamy Iyer served as Diwan from 1936 to 1947; during his tenure, many social and administrative reforms were made. However, at the same time, he is also remembered for the ruthless suppression of the communist-organized Punnapra-Vayalar revolt, and his controversial stand in favor of an independent Travancore. He resigned in 1947 following a failed assassination attempt. He served as a leader of the Indian National Congress in his early days. He was made a Knight Commander of the Indian Empire in 1926 and a Knight Commander of the Star of India in 1941. He returned these titles when India attained independence in 1947. He was also a member of the 1926 and 1927 delegations to the League of Nations. In his later life he served in numerous international organizations and on the board of several Indian universities. Ramaswamy Iyer died in 1966 at the age of 86 while on a visit to the United Kingdom.

As a Member of the Executive Council of the Governor of Madras

A sketch of Sir C. P. Ramaswamy Iyer in a London newspaper during the Third Round Table Conference

As a member of the executive council, C. P. laid the foundation of the Pykara Dam, which was constructed between 1929 and 1932 at a cost of Rs. 67.5 million. He also started the construction of the Mettur Dam over the Cauvery River. While the Pykara Hydro-electric project triggered the rapid industrialization of Coimbatore, the Mettur project was used to irrigate vast areas of the Tanjore and Trichy districts. As the member in charge of ports, C. P. was also responsible for the improvement of the Cochin, Visakhapatnam and Tuticorin ports.

Between 1926 and 1927 he was the Indian Delegate at the League of Nations in Geneva. By 1931 he was a Law Member] of the Government of India, and in 1932 attended the Third Round Table Conference in London. In 1933 he was the sole] Indian delegate to the World Economic Conference and the next year he drafted a constitution for the state of Kashmir"

Diwan of Travancore

Economic and Industrial Reforms

Master Builder

"He was builder of dams, canals, hydroelectric works, fertilizer plants, member of Viceroy's executive council, vice-chancellor of three universities, delegate at the third round table conference and much more"

~ Khushwant Singh, Master Builder, 17 July 1999

During C. P.'s tenure as Diwan, Travancore made rapid strides in industrial development. The Indian Aluminum Company was invited to set up a factory in the town of Aluva. The first fertilizer plant in India, the Fertilizers and Chemicals of Travancore Ltd. (FACT) was established by C. P. to manufacture ammonium sulphate This was established with American collaboration in open defiance to the hostility of the Viceroy of India. C.P. also established a plant to manufacture cement and another to manufacture titanium dioxide. The Travancore plywood factory at Punalur The Travancore Rayons Limited was established in 1946 with a plant at Perumbavoor.[35] The first plant to manufacture aluminum cables was opened at Kundara. By the time, C. P. stepped down as Diwan in 1947, the revenues of the state had increased fourfold from the time he had assumed charge.

Punnapra-Vayalar Revolt

See also: Punnapra-Vayalar uprising

A mass uprising broke out in the Alleppey region in October 1946. On 24 October Travancore police killed nearby about 200 people in Punnapra and the government ordered martial law in Alleppey and Cherthala. C .P's police and army moved to Alleppey and on 27 October, Vayalar witnessed another mass uprising as 150 people were killed on the spot. On the same day 130 people were killed in different locations of Alleppey in police shoot-outs. According to Prof. A Shreedhara Menon's Kerala History, about 1,000 people died in the Punnapra Vayalar Agitation. Even though the agitation was a short-lived failure, it resulted in a better administration of Travancore.

Declaration of Independence

On June 3, 1947, the United Kingdom accepted demands for a partition and announced its intention to quit India within a short period, and Maharaja of Travancore desired to declare himself Independent. Supported by the Diwan, C. P., Chithira Thirunal issued a Declaration of independence on June 18, 1947. As Travancore's Declaration of Independence was unacceptable to India, negotiations were started with the Diwan by the Government of India. Family sources indicate that C. P. himself was not in favor of independence but only greater autonomy, and that a favorable agreement had been reached between C. P. and the Indian representatives by July, 23, 1947 however, accession to the Indian Union could not be carried out only because it was pending approval by the Raja. On the other hand, noted historian Ramachandra Guha has written about how C. P., egged on by Mohammed Ali Jinnah, had established secret ties with senior Ministers of the British Government, who encouraged him in the hope that he would give them privileged access to monazite, a material Travancore was rich in and which could give the British a lead in the nuclear arms race. Nevertheless, an assassination attempt was made on C. P. on 25 July 1947 during a concert commemorating the anniversary of Swati Thirunal. C. P. survived with multiple stab wounds and hastened the accession of Travancore state to the Indian Union soon after his recovery

Later Years

After he resigned his Diwanship of Travancore, C. P. left for London. In the same year, he visited Brazil on the invitation of the Government of Brazil and Argentina, Peru and Mexico as a tourist. He also visited the United States of America where he gave talks at the University of California, Berkeley, and had discussions with important bank executives, journalists and US President Harry S. Truman. In 1949–50, he visited the United States again as a visiting professor of the American Academy of Asian Studies at California. In 1952, he toured Australia and New Zealand as a guest of the respective governments and visited the United States again in 1953 on a lecture tour. From 1 July 1954 to 2 July 1956, he served as the Vice Chancellor of Banaras Hindu University. From 26 January 1955, C. P. also served as a Vice Chancellor of Annamalai University, thereby becoming the first Indian to function as Vice Chancellor of two universities at the same time. In 1953, C.P. was appointed member of the Press Commission of India. Two years later, C. P. toured China as the leader of an Indian university's delegation.

In conclusion I am quoting a section written by R.V. Rajan on the biography of C. P . by A Raghu" The life of C P. Ramaswamy Aiyar"

"Travancore under CP pioneered many social measures: untouchability was done away with through direct governmental action, capital punishment was abolished, a free midday meal scheme for schoolchildren was introduced, and agricultural income tax levied. Countering opposition to the idea, the University of Travancore was inaugurated its 1937.

Free and compulsory primary education was introduced throughout the State, with handicrafts, music and physical training included in the curriculum. The industrialization of Travancore also proceeded apace".

C P Mathen and Travancore and Quilon Bank

The Kerala history won't be complete without major historical events from 1900 - 1947.

https://en.wikipedia.org/wiki/Travancore_National_and_Quilon_Bank

The rise and fall of TNQ bank, Amol Agrawal, Chalakuzhy Paulose Mathen

(Business and journalism are a bad mix with politics. Malayala Manorama owner Mammem Mappilai and banking leader C. P. Mathen supported protests and agitation against the government. We know from history that everywhere in the world, governments use subtle methods to silence the opposition in every age. Even in America after 2015 the government and FBI colluded with technology companies to suppress the opposition. This is a basic human nature. So, we can see that CP Ramaswamy Iyer destroyed his opposition. The bank failure was a great blow for the Kerala economy and destroyed the backbone of the Christian community.)

C P. Mathen (May 18, 1890 June 2, 1960), Chalakuzhy Paulose Mathen was an Indian politician who served as Member of the Indian Parliament in the first Lok Sabha, constituted in 1952 after India gained independence from Great Britain. He represented the Tiruvalla constituency of Kerala. Mathen was appointed the Indian Ambassador to Sudan after his single term in the Lok Sabha. Before his entry into politics, Mathen was a businessman with interests in cashew, minerals, insurance, plantations and banking. He was responsible for starting the Alleppey Chamber of Commerce. He was Managing Director of the Travancore National and Quilon Bank (TN&Q Bank) when it suffered a run of unprecedented length that forced it to close. The bank run was said to have been escalated by Sir C. P. Ramaswamy Iyer] the Diwan of Travancore, in an attempt to reduce the power of the Christian Community who were agitating for fair representation in the governing council of this Princely State. C.P. Mathen was extradited from Madras and imprisoned in Trivandrum, allegedly for balance sheet irregularities. He was sentenced to rigorous imprisonment but offered many chances to walk free if he would acknowledge guilt. C.P. Mathen refused these offers, maintaining his innocence for more than three years. He became something of a folk hero for his uncompromising stand. He was released on January 22, 1942 without condition or explanation and returned to Madras.

Early life: Insurance and Banking

At the age of 29, Mathen raised Rs 56,000 in capital and Rs 54,000 in deposits and started a bank that he called the Quilon Bank with its headquarters in Kollam (Quilon), The Quilon Bank headquarter building was then constructed and completed in 1935. In a relatively short space of 15 years, the bank's total working capital rose from Rs 156,000 to Rs 10,246,000.

Another leading Travancore businessman of that era was Mr. K.C. Mammen Mappillai, whose interests were not only in banking - his bank was called the Travancore National Bank - but also in journalism, newspaper publishing and politics. His heart was actually in journalism, and he was the Chief Editor of a Travancore newspaper, Malayala Manorama.

Mammen and Mathen had started an insurance company together, and the commercial success of this new venture led them to amalgamate their respective banks in 1937. The registered office remained at the Quilon Bank headquarters in Travancore but the main business of the bank was conducted from its central office in Madras where its primary shareholders were based. Sir CP Ramaswamy Iyer,] encouraged this arrangement by offering to place Rs 7,000,000 of Travancore treasury money with the merged bank but this offer was never fulfilled.

The TN&Q Bank was the fourth-largest bank in India and the largest in South India. It had 75 branches in British India, Travancore, Cochin, and Malabar,

Imprisonment

TN&Q Bank was established in 1937 with a new Quilon headquarters building which Mathen built at a cost of Rs. 140,000 (a very large sum of money at that time). To retain the business and deposits of the Travancore State, Mathen and Mammen had not only agreed to the headquarters in Travancore but that two of the bank's directors were the Diwan's appointees and also that the Bank's General Manager, a confidant of the Diwan named K. S. Ramanujam, was appointed at the specific recommendation of Sir CP. Despite this initial support from the Travancore Government, within a few months of amalgamation being completed, rumors started making its rounds that the bank was insolvent, and by 1938 there was a run on the bank's assets – this was instigated not only by the Diwan but was publicized by the Travancore State's Department of Publicity. The bank's financial run concluded with 88% of the public's deposits being returned by the bank, and the bank becoming insolvent. At this point the trap was sprung, by Sir CP's administration demanding the extradition of Mathen and Mammen from Madras Presidency to Travancore State to stand trial for defrauding the public. Sir CP also convinced the British Government in Madras that the bank and its directors had been financing the Congress party and the Independence movement. He appeals to the Madras High Court and the Privy Council in London to stay the extradition orders were rejected and 4 directors of the bank including Mathen, Mammen and Mammen's elder brother and Mammen's son, were transported in chains from Madras to Quilon to stand trial.

At the trial in Trivandrum, the erstwhile General Manager of the bank - K. S. Ramanujam, who was the nominee of the Maharaja's government - falsely testified that Mammen and Mathen had defrauded the bank and four directors (including Mammen's brother and son) were then awarded 8 years' imprisonment. The bank's remaining assets were liquidated by the State, and the bank's assets were distributed - mainly to confidants of Sir C. P. Ramaswamy Iyer, one of whom acquired the bank headquarters' building in Quilon for Rs 15,000 - approximately a tenth of what it had cost to build three years earlier. With the first year in jail, Mammen's imprisoned elder brother died a broken man. Soon afterwards, Sir CP, who had been an astute lawyer in the colonial administration, being keenly aware of the weaknesses in the Government's case – which depended on K. S. Ramanujam who vanished abroad after the trial - sent word to Mammen and Mathen that if they admitted their accused guilt and sought the Maharaja's mercy they could be pardoned. Mammen and his son, had other major family problems, so they agreed to sign the false declaration but Mathen continued to refuse. Sir CP initially declined to agree to the release without all of three of them admitting guilt, but finally released Mammen and his son on receiving their written "confessions". Mathen continued to hold out on his refusal to sign any false confession, despite heavy pressure brought on him through the Inspector General of Police, Mr Abdul Karim, visiting him regularly in jail and suggesting that he sign a letter – which the IG had drafted, requesting the Maharaja to pardon and release him. Finally, on 22 January 1942, Mr. C. P. Mathen was unconditionally released by the Maharaja's Government without any written or verbal false admission of guilt. The IG, Mr. Abdul Karim, took Mathen in his official car from Travancore jail to his house where his family had waited patiently for his release from jail.

Mr. C. P. Mathen was a member of the First Lok Sabha (Indian Parliament) in 1952, representing Tiruvalla Constituency of Kerala.

Lok Sabha Member and Ambassador

He was elected to the first Lok Sabha in 1953, from Mavelikera constitutioncy in Kerala by one of the largest majorities of that election.

After completing his term in the Lok Sabha, in 1957, he was appointed as the Indian Ambassador to Sudan. He retired a year later due to health reasons caused by his years of imprisonment in Trivandrum.

Death

C. P. Mathen died on June 2, 1960, in Paris, -France, and he was buried at Tiruvalla, Kerala, India.

Appendix

Sabir Ali, Bangalore.

Kerala Christians and Their Names

Before I landed in a new country for cross-culture Missions, my real cross- culture Missions training started in Kerala. My passion to get into the Bible college brought me from remote North India to South India's Kerala Pathnammthitta. I grew up with mustard oil and suddenly my whole taste was changed to coconut oil. Each day I had a new experience. The most difficult part for me was to pronounce some of the places of Kerala, and some of their names and what they call house name. I found three types of names: The first is Biblical like John, Mathew, Mark, and Thomas, the second types of names were Varghese, Chakco, Parakal, etc., and the third Type of names were Shiju, Bijju, Sajju and . Saji. It was very confusing, and I wanted to know more about name development.

One of the very prominent and learned scholars in the Brethren circle is Dr. John Matthew, and I approached him to tell me the history behind such names. He is an encyclopedia and can be approached anytime for any information. And here He writes:

Sabir - As promised I am going to provide some historical perspectives of Kerala Christians and their names.

This is from my research in Sociology. You were confused with me and Mathew John. Most Kerala Christians gave names only from the Bible until around the 1960s.

So, wherever we gather there will be confusion. In Houston, there is a famous John Mathew. He belongs to the Church of South India, an Anglican version. We both are very famous among secular Malayalees in Kerala and North America. So, people called me on the phone thinking that it was the other John Mathew. He also used to get calls intended for me. Therefore, in the early nineties I decided to accept my pen name as Sunny Ezhumattoor. Ezhumattoor is the village where I was born. Usually, writers and public figures are known by the name of their birthplace, like Jesus of Nazareth. This way we both escaped our the problem. In a Malayalee gathering you can see numerous names such as   Thomas Mathew, John Mathew, Varghese John, Abraham Daniel etc. Most Indians are followers. Although Malayalees think that they are born leaders, they are also followers.

Most Malayalee youth went to foreign countries for employment. They wanted to display their new fashions, styles and behaviors. They began to name their children with fancy names to get attention. The first few syllables or the last syllable of names are similar sounding (rhyming). For example: Sijo, Lijo, Anjo, Panjo, Banjo, Tony, Tikky,

Timmy, Tinny, Finny, Minni, Kinny, Chinny, Litty and Kitty.

First child-Anish, second child-Binish, third child Cinish and the next child was their last and they called the child FINISH!

Most names have no meaning. Most of these parents are narcissists. Some parents select a combination of both mother's and Father's names. Ex: Suresh and Sharon= Susha; Joseph and Beena= Jobi. Soje means son of John and Elizabeth. Doje = daughter of John and Elizabeth. Toje= third child of John and Elizabeth.

Thanku is the son of Thankamma and Kunjumon. Also, these vainglorious parents used to make a loud statement that their children did not speak Malayalam, but only English.

Something strange happened thirty years ago in the Cochin area. The neighbor who was employed in the Middle East named their children, Litty and Mitty. An uneducated lady who lived next door named her daughter Shitty. When her cousin visited from the USA and asked the baby's name, she told him that it was shitty. In shock the cousin explained the meaning and asked her to change the baby's name.

In my bank employment the year before I retired my investment banker came and asked me, " John, I had a client today and his last name is also Mathew. He may be related to you, however his first name is strange. It is Titty. Why do you people give such weird names"? Sabir, you know that Tit is the colloquial word or meaning for breast. I told him that in India one time they used to give such foolish names ignorantly.

Although Titty Mathew was a medical doctor, he didn't change his name.

However, Hindus had a better value system. They all have their traditional names such as Anil Kumar, Lalitha, Karunakaran etc.

I hope this will give you a picture of how such names developed. I have written many essays on such subjects in Malayalam.

Dr. John Matthew

OBJECTIVE OF THIS POST - JUST FOR SOCIOLOGICAL INFORMATION ...

9 798390 861196